imaginary truths

avi sato

springwaterspress

for robert and jean

who held my head above the waves

when i had forgotten how to swim

water

a stream breaks
the stillness of the forest
always having been there
just beneath the icy surface
but slightly outside the doors of my mind's
      awareness
with each footstep drawing closer
and suddenly shattering the veil
of subtle ignorance
i had built between us

in the moon's absence
darkness implies a distance
i know is purely imagined
in the echoes of unstillness
yet somehow i choose to believe
in the feeling of loneliness
i drink as an elixir
after a lifetime of noise
i can suddenly shut out

with birdsong's shivering in the almost stillness

starlight is pierced by sudden movement
a hair's width from my vision
and light explodes
blurring all
but the most rudimentary of shapes
as i dizzily stare
into what once was gentle shadow
and now shimmers in flame's heat

i sang once as a child
of bright golden orbs descending
from a heaven built for the young
and normal
so those who fear at night may sleep
and pretend life ends
with beginnings
filled with sunlights undimmed
and chantings of worship

yet when it comes

i discover a fear it neither subdued nor preempted

in its artifice of whitened beards

and priestly robes

wings of folded silk

and gospel hymns implied

and all too human

while my head spins

in meteoric anticipation of new fires

beyond comfortable closeness

heat stings not my face

but my mind

as i pick up my feet

from their collapsed failings

and beat them into the group

loosely concentrating on outrunning the star

newly touched on an earth

both unsuspecting and shallowly prepared

fires' tongues lick my eyes

from above

and below

as trees give themselves bodily

to a miniaturized armageddon

that moments before was nothing

but my mind's projected stillness

on a landscape

minding everything's business but my own

plunging

into that icy stream

as fiery songs scream harsh curses above me

i give myself totally to the beauty of cold

radiating through me

not as the stiffness i imagined

but freedom

while heat reverberates above

i break the surface from below

gasping from lungs' unintelligible depths

and smile

dripping from the forest's impromptu sauna

face blackened but thankful

for a survival i hadn't guessed could be in question

until this instant

i drink deeply of burned air
and walk slowly
laughing from the other bank
safe into a morning
not yet beginning
to break
but of a day
scented with extraterrestrial incense
and the birthday candles
of a life only just begun anew

never

you

who cares but a moment

for the fallen child

whose eyes aflame with waters of sadness

cries unmistakable animal screams

that mingle in an air of passionate hatred

and holds

between your hands and theirs

the beauty of a smile

newly applied to face

just instants before a mask of sorrow

casting itself into futures

now lost

you

whose fingers touch the once-reflective streams

where surface beneath the stars

competed with its mysterious depths

but no longer

from its imperfect form

echoes anything

but society's impassioned disregard

for all but its own momentary bliss

yet your words

and voices

and loves

and trees

placed between hands

between souls

between us

and a nature we forgot to protect

you gave new life

where once life sprung

you

whose eyes breathed imperfect futures

where only pasts existed

within pages of stories long forgotten

for children

whose ears were turned away

from all but excitement and noise

yet within you

a love of thought

and letter

and sounds

not loud but fracturing

in their whispered stillness

shook from their contemplations

those lust-ridden adults

teaching their children to close their ears

and minds

and hearts

and eyes

and in you they see a hope

taught all their yet-short lives

was more extinct

than species their parents killed

to keep their world

from embracing the change

they once proclaimed

on streets that ran with blood

and now are paved with blackened gold

in them

your image shines

against a backdrop of compassionate tenderness

yet you notice not

as you have simply moved on

to hold another tear-streaked world

between your hands

and speak life through its breath

kiss

a candle flame in darkness
is consumed by the night
and in your face i see the reflection
of the hope you lost long ago
yet conjure up in me with each glance

a silver tongue of light
in the predawn black
tastes within my eyes
the shadow of our time together
cut short by my failure and your beautiful memory
living now only within my mind's shortcomings

a voice of laughter imagines itself
from behind my unseeing hallucinations
yet you are here with me
just out of my line of sight
carefully composing yourself
between sheets and pillows

to surprise me in my sleep

i feel your touch

on the skin of my dreams

as you reach from behind reality's blindspot

to hold me

as once i could have returned in kind

but the distance of eons

spreads between us in endings

you tell me in secret whisperings

that you have gone nowhere

that you are here and now and always

within my reach

but with each movement of my hands

i feel nothing

but the fire of your energy

and see the smoke of your form

turn to dust

over my shoulder

as i turn to drink in your reality

we are not separate you say

and i hear its echo

without the words having been spoken into the

      room

and i have spent so many years

pretending to believe you

that i no longer resist its truth

you sing of enlightenment

yet i think it a joke

as no weight is here beside me

in the stillness of linen

and the shifting of my shivering form

touches the floor

before meeting any resistance

from a body once yours

and now ash

but in the stillness

i finally feel the unreality of myself

as i stop looking for you to return

and for me to move forward

to meet you there

as once i thought

i would need rope and tree and sadness to achieve

the voice i once thought

mocking in its distant proximity

calls me to know

you are not far but in me

not only as memory

but a force just as strong as mine

a nature of breathing this moment

my hands touch an earth

where you are no longer missing

and in the first moment of dawn

i raise my eyes from the morning's cold tatami

and kiss you once again

as you merge with the sunlight

to warm my face

mirrors

lost in escapist dreams

i cover my face

with hands whose eyes look only inward

and swallow bitter futures

tasting of lemon-flavored tears

whose words can echo in the sunlight

and not be overwhelmed

by the unspoken desire

to penetrate not their depths

but their performances

and carry you

to be fucked before cave paintings

and discarded

at the mouth of the desecrated temple

who will cover your sinful transgressions

with a white robe

and gather your remains to be resurrected

as you awaken

before altered realities

will your ears hear new birdsong
teaching melodies you once forgot
in your search for untruth and lust
when you crawled across mattresses
in the simulated darkness
toward falling towers of fire

or is collapse the end of ages still young
and promises unbroken
while spirits' followers encircle
the trees of your forest-dwelling mind
and chant curses on your name

are you willing to stand naked on the path
between heaven's gates
and cry for help
or is shame the lifeblood of secrecy

will your skin once again be cleaned
by the afternoon winds

as you kneel

to speak your promises

to ears no longer deaf

as your absent dreams return to your breath

and smile

through lips hovering in the flickering candles

as you gather yourselves

as one body

and light the fuze of an explosion

until today you thought would only arrive

from acts of pretended passion

will you bow to yourself in respect

or cry new oaths of self-loathing

and run from your own reflection

to hide in a home you forget

is built from glass

as all you see are mirrors

shimmering with endless selfie failures

and burrow more deeply

into blanket fortresses

built to repel all but the borders of your life

where all may cross

until new value is found within

and you learn to speak negatives of truth

against proclamations of faked entreaties of

      hopeless matrimony

do eyes open to see through still lakes that

      surround your form

as you walk from pillows' assumptions

between doorposts

into the familiar sunshine

today you may rest

but will tonight's stars rise on you

in the strength of knowledge

will tomorrow wake to your promised hope

and taste smiles on your lips

eyes

i lost myself in your eyes

and into that depth i fell

not as a stone

but a feather

floating ever closer

yet never reaching a place where i could rest

i heard words of derision from my own lips

echoed back at me

from the walls of the cavern

and i tasted nothing

but the salt of my own tears

flowing in the rivers

whose life i tried to drink

to sustain me in the burning winds

if you were there and heard my cries

you were silent

and unmoved

by the sound and i felt no arms hold me

as my panic stirred deeper within my skin

the touch of water turned to floods
as my feet tripped on the polished rocks
whose surfaces showed only blackened reflections
of my still-darker self

with each droplet
i cringed as my face fell
toward the surface
yet it receded just beyond my reach
and before my thankfulness for safety could grow
i once again plunged in its direction

the endless cycles numbed me
to a hope i already knew had long since walked
      away
and climbed to peaks of mountains
in someone else's life

but i no longer felt alone
in the compassion of your eyes

and into their stirring grayness

i cast myself

looking for a stillness to lose myself in

and in those glassy spheres

i thought for a moment

whose existence i only caught

out of the corner of my blinded eyes

i could taste the strength

to climb the day's path

and feel myself again

yet it was but an instant too late

when i discovered the eyes whose hope i fell into

looked startlingly familiar

in my newfound clarity

the mirror shattered as i touched its face

and no longer was i lost but broken

as i tasted its lifeless glass

standing

within my head

a solemn drum counts seconds

as i drift between wakefulness

and a loss of control

i fear will consume me

and wish would save me

from the self

that tears me apart

by day

and clenches the fists of teeth

that hold me upright

at night

rainfall beats patterns

too complex for earthly drummers

on pitchless surfaces

just outside my mind's contemplative reach

yet in their distance

they call to me

to walk away from thought

and drink their hopeful sounds
of happy repetition

if only i could lift myself
from the prison
i have created
in my own image
a safety
lost in its own endeavors
and walk
a single step
toward the source of the rain
and hold it within my fingers
as it slips endlessly away
drinking me
as would i hold it against my lips

were i only spirit
i would float
between the bounds
of one droplet on the breeze
and follow it

through its dances with leaves

until it forgets

to keep itself

separate

from all it touches

and disappears

without losing its identity

within the stream

flowing to oceans

in an endless parade of undiscovery

would you hold my droplet

and keep it safe

as i

within it deeply search

for the embrace of one

who can always

break me

apart

but chooses instead to shelter me

from plunging into the sea

of my own making

to lose myself

in the maze of mindless self-control and

boundaries

achieving nothing

but holding me

back

from pain that arrives anyway

you who sees the fear

in my shivering eyes

and has not run

toward those streams

to walk through

and climb the mountain on the other side

to escape the clutch

of my panicked fingers

while i barely notice your presence

watching me

with unconcealed emotions

of sadness

and pity

and doubt

and hope for a change

i know i cannot embrace

even if i knew

from what direction it would arrive

or could place

a word

a name

a thought

a single idea on it

and call it

scream it into existence

and back out again

as the dark force

i feel it to be deep in my fear

as feeling things in my heart

is something

i have long since forgotten how to do

but you are standing

and that in itself is

something i have barely comprehended

as the others forgot themselves

and only saw the self i created

to mirror them

and i am here

not standing but curled

as childlike

i return to the fear of infant

and curiosity of youth

with the answers of adulthood

and none of the right questions

so with each answer

comes new silky folds

of shimmering panic

and endless clothes of attention

drawn to secret shames of sickness

in which i wrap myself

as were they silver wings

and halos of fine jade

your eyes take in

my moments of darkness

and see in an instant

they span a lifetime

and reach your fingers to me

in forgiveness

as i

shrink

from your touch

and make to escape

yet in that second of flinching terror

you pause and reassure

with voice

and text

and song

and air that distance is something to be held

and i am safe without flight

i reach for your hand

and stop

as fingers do not quite touch

yet you understand that contact

as the first step

toward a love you already know is there

and in me i feel nothing

but the torture from within my head

but know without a question

the first doubtless thought i have breathed

in time undefined

i may not be safe

but i am

yours

second

i do not taste the rain

as i open my mouth

and watch the wind

carry its beautiful clarity

a safety i wish i could create

within myself

and drink its pure simplicity

in my life of contaminated ideas

and liquid loss of self-control

but i should not be surprised

as i am shielded

from the water

by window

and wall

and in this prison i have created

for myself

i feel nothing

but more myself forgotten

by the goddesses of health

i pray to day and night

in hope
they will save me from myself
a human lost
to each moment
by my own hatred
of a body not just my own
but each of ours
in a disgust
not paralleled
even in the death we see
in others' lifeless forms
as they are somehow cleaner in their end
than i could be in my beginning
not quite finished in its sickness

i am broken
clinging to a life i thought
would be the defining of myself
but only describing the arcs
of bodies colliding

less and less

with each other

in their unheavenly paths

and broken

not just as a word to describe myself

but one to shatter interactions

as i place roadblocks

around me

to keep

myself

alone

as in the pain of loneliness

the pain of humanity

is lessened or so i once believed

and repeat to myself

as the undying mantra of my religion

where i worship the spirit of unsensed peace

yet a war rages within

the depths

and you see

and hear

and feel nothing of it

until i open my mouth and cry

the names

i hold within me

of a hatred

born not of human love

but a terror to shake not limbs but trunks

and i turn

and shiver

as i try to run

but get nowhere

since there is no place

where i can escape myself

and with each footstep

i gain distance from the past

but draw closer

not to a future i fear

but a present i abhor

and can reach back into myself

and touch again

and again

building it into a demon

that may not even have existed

were it not for me calling its name

but into a dark self

i pour the shimmering fear of reflections

on the oil-soaked water

of karma unrequited

and love

not strong enough to carry me

as i have turned from its soft lyrics

too many times

for them to hold more than an echo

of their former selves

weak as a single teardrop

diluted in a river of sediment

and leaves

pressing endlessly

toward an ocean of self-consumption

do you hear the voices screaming

behind my eyes

the repetition with each heartbeat

of the truths i hoped were lies

what happens if i fail

to clean myself

and each vicious attack is not subverted

with the application of distance

and water

and heat

and moments of gasped breathing

where i am frightened to take in any

but the smallest breath

a lie in its promise of life

as its oxygen holds itself

away from me

in my terror

for fear

that in that breath

may come the darkness of contamination

and shame

of pressing self into the world

from within

without my consent

or control

or hope of returning to a stable self

when parts of what once were within

are now on display

and my body is broken in my eyes and yours

by a fate far worse than the death of ritual

or by a hand that may be mine

or yours

were you willing

to help me end the fear

by the only means

i can describe to you

in words

and why

in all the spoken loves you give

does the one act i long for

stay so helplessly out of reach

and life continues

with each

gasped

breath

and you tell me i am safe

when i know you cannot possibly read

the tortured cells inside me

screaming to escape

and create new nightmares

with each

passing

second

and failed secret swallowing of self-control

a second has passed and for me it is a lifetime

but you have not moved

and i have no idea

if it is because you are here

for me

or if a second feels like nothing at all to you

but somehow you smile

and the difference could not matter less

yet another second has begun

and into its time

i pour my contaminated thoughts

and begin again the cycle

with

scandal wakes me

yet i have not even for a second

fallen asleep

and i know all too well that the darkness i see

is because i have closed my eyes

and it is not just daylight that is outside me

but the voices of so many people

whose bodies quiver with unpredicted sickness

were i to open myself to see it again

but i have lost the fight for yet another day

as i see them in my mind

and need not take in any more senses

that i wish so dearly would simply end

and leave me to feel nothing

but the death i have never desired

but always knew would have to come some day

to save me from the prison of lies and truth

unbroken from each other

that i have built around my body

and inside my head

it was the momentary twitch
of breath
and head
and hand on stomach
that made me feel the depths of myself
plummet toward the floor
and captured nothing of the saving power of finger
and hands
and feet allowing me to stand
or sit
or catch myself as i fall

but i can say with certainty
that humans when they drop to stone
do not at all behave like balls
as much as we may wish it to be the case
and bounce
but simply break
but not enough to end the panic that lives
deep inside my spirit

but has no difficulty expressing itself

with each passing minute of my life

i do not know how long the darkness lasted

but only that i wish

from deepest hearts long lost to fear's torture

that it could have been not longer

but always

and then i would have no reason to return

to the place where things have changed

in ways i cannot put back in their box

and send to those i wish

would take them in their arms

they speak the tortured words of questions

that i wish would not be asked the

are you oks

and panted breathing

mere centimeters from my face

unprotected in its unmasked existence

and wonder why i cannot bring myself to open my

      eyes

if they could only leave

and not put themselves too close

and touch

and breathe

and speak proximities

and urgencies

and tensions

that do nothing but fuel the abject panic that

      made me fall

and sadly saved my head from stoned collapse

by the sheer suddenness of vertical descent

as legs cushioned me

in their folding

perhaps

if i could open just an eye

i could make them walk away

but in the effort nothing comes but blackness

and i think that in a way better

i close the eyes that were never opened
and return to absence
only to wake anew in a future i hope never appears
when i shall have no choice but to live

again

preparation

it's the precautions that kill me

not the anticipation

though that is certainly a part of my life

the knowledge that not in the future

but in this moment

here

and now

and this

and without my knowledge

except for the unquestioning certainty within my

    spirit

that i will drop to knees and lose myself

as liquid

becomes less me and more outside myself

and i no longer hold rigid control

of a self lost in that instant to a future

outside my wildest nightmares

yet that is the domain of each

for nighttimes lasting hours

are days of endless self as victim

of my own mistakes

but that aside

the pain of preparation

is the source of each imagined future

wherein i lose myself

and only stand to grasp the knife i wish were there

but must in my self-loss find

to simplify the end

that i knew would always have to come in such a

     moment

of shameful freedom of the self within

to prepare

in case there is a shift in what i can control

and what i can predict

and what i have let invade my body

and my mind

and hopefully not my spirit

but there is always that potential i suppose

where endless lives

and not just this one

may be destroyed

and made to be much more than simple suffering

but terror

conveyed with each passing breath

and touch

and taste

and feeling that another is there with me

to communicate not hope and love

or maybe those as well

but first and foremost only hatred

not from that other

but from the miniature lives that populate their

      breaths

and land on me from far

and closer still their touch on me

or else the touch of them

on something that i have not seen

before my hand accidentally reaches for it

an action that i sometimes cannot help but fall

      into the trap of doing to myself

do i leave this here

or put that there

or just in case there is a failure of myself

and that i need to have something set up for when

     i fall

and fail

and collapse into that future

that i simply wait to come

with each single captured breath

and know that i will thankfully not survive for

     long

before i finally give in to death

and let it come

and claim my body

and release my spirit to inhabit any life that

oh i pray

will not have such a terrorized existence

as the one that i find myself trapped in at this

     moment

you tell me

i am safe

but i know it is only your way of telling me

that i should be calm

with the urgency of calmlessness that you have

      learned

from the expectation that my panic never ends

and creates in you a terror much the same

that i wish so thoroughly

with each gasped breath

i could take away from you

yet no idea comes of how to do for either of us

i am nothing if not sorry

and in these preparations

i collapse into a future

i only hope does not consume all those i love

but fear it has already

come

where are you oh delightful muse

i whisper my words
into the stillness i have created here for myself
sitting alone
with headphones
to block out the reality i only wish would
      disappear
and stop haunting my days

it is only early morning
and lazy sunshine casts its grayness
across another bleak
windswept scene
that i have summarily erased with curtains
to turn fall colors to christmas
with dreams of spices
and sounds of brass carols

i wish away the time

and thought

with each passing daybreak

and collapse into myself

in search not of you

dear muse

but of the person i once was

whose morning rituals were all too ordinary

before fear and questions of if

and when

and how badly i will fall

consumed my reality

and powders swallowed as lifeblood

dominated a future

that was nothing but past

and passing

with a rapidity like birthdays

coming every month

old i see in the mirror

while others

when rarely i let them see

speak words of youth

and i feel nothing but closer to the certainty of

　　　death

with each second stretching hours

and days as lifetimes

amid a failure to act

so in your disappearance

you hurt me far less than you dream

as there is nothing left to fear

that i do not dwell endlessly on

and an absence of words

is far more pleasant

than a loss of self in each moment

to the racks of uncontrolled panic

in the face of contagion

but in my moments of inquiry

i beg you to return

beautiful muse

and touch in me the inspiration

that may turn me from dejected corpse

walking with the loss of me

that i write into being

and out of it again

before the eyes of those who think it must be only

     persona

for their voyeuristic schadenfreude

tell them it is my truth

and in their lies i find no solace

but in their tears there is a joy

for them to discover in their thankfulness

that's this horror has not infected their lives

as within me it rages

as perfected storm

within an endlessly shattering bottle

then come back to me

and taste in my fingertips

a poem of love for the few

who hold me in their dreams

and desires

and cares

so i may soothe them

as they have tried

with so many words to do in me

and failed

time

and time

and minutes again

as they are dear to me

but the notes of your twisted words

are nothing but the diamond in the ring i present

        to them

and would it be a gift

worth the name of song

requiem

death doesn't hunt in the night

but in the bright expanse of sunlit plains

where we stand happily

oblivious of its dangers

but in that moment of sudden falling

we reach out

with helpless hands

to press away the ground

rushing up to meet us in the shimmering haze of

      afternoon brilliance

and ask the stunned question

of where the mask of darkness was hiding in the

      clear sky

no warning is heeded

but in the crystalline afterglow

we see its face

clearly taunting us

through the hazy pasts of dancing

in a world of peaceful covers over simmering
       hatreds

the gunshots
echoing in the distance
are frighteningly close
as we walk through the pillars of school doorways
and out the classrooms of our minds
without the slightest understanding
our backs are no longer against the walls
that shield us from the traitor's bullet

we are outsiders
in a world where thought is the enemy
and equality is a diversionary tactic
for those who wish to divide
the rulers
and drink someone else's blackened gold
or paint their perfect nails in stolen blood

i curl into a childish ball
here among the grasses

and look up at the sanctuary of a mountain in the
        distance
i can never reach
to climb my own inverted olympus moment
ascending in the far-off unrealities
of a future yet to fall on my head

but again
i am told to stand tall
to face the enemies from outside
that are just like us
in all but pretended names
and languages without meaning
in their babbling nationalism

together
is a word with forgotten hopes
and liquid dreams
poured into polluted rivers

as the front draws closer
and i am backed into a corner of false starts

hold my hand

as you march against the crowd

into the wilderness

whose mirrors are long since shattered

and dive into the pure waters of glacier melt

to let their icy depths purify our souls once again

and shut out the fiery present

given to us by those who preach words of salvation

from altered truths

on human mountains

robins

in childhood dusk

i saw an elderly lady

feeding robins by the side of a lake

and sat to watch

until she walked out of my line of sight

i thought nothing of the encounter at the time

but smiled for days

after at the beauty of a simple act of kindness

among the barren winter winds

for so many tiny lives that would have disappeared

were it not for her

together

was always a thought i had such difficulty with

among days of competition

and being told to believe in

and rely on

and depend on

and hope for myself

from days of classes ranked by grade
to nights of fighting demons
alone in my dreams
to dawns of silent solitude
wishing i could be far from the noise of the
        classroom

then i remembered the robins
and knew that this was a better life
one of momentary perfection
in the smiles they gave her
and pleasure she poured out in return
a mutual rainbow

and in the mirror
i saw the smiles i had achieved
from that ordinary kindness
and understood that i was not outside watching
but participating in the exchange of hope
as she looked

and smiled at me

and drank in the simple joy

of making another smile

within the world of self and other

collapsing into the unity that we all feel

if only we are prepared to listen to it speak in our

       hearts

over the noise of our minds

and here in my daydreams

i wonder where they have gone

those pieces of my life

i have never forgotten

long departed from this world

but not taken from my dreams

i know now what it means

never to die

trip

a beauty overwhelms me

but i cannot remember it

as my eyes have been closed for so long

against the terror of the night

that the day is

nothing

but a burning sphere

etching itself into my mind

is you

the point where fickle imagination

meets fuzzy memory

or are you a goddess become human

for only this moment

to dance at the edge of my consciousness

as i walk by

never to repeat this instant again

i find my feet suddenly wet

as i distracted walk into the bed of a once-dry

    stream

now overflowing with rebuilt tastes of the past

and water from a glacier

whose tongue has brushed against humanity

once too often

for even amida to pull its forever-chanting self

out of the guilty fingers of presidential

    overreaching

i gasp

but you don't turn your head quickly

and i know you have been watching all along

but only slightly

as the laughter from your solitary imaginings

ripples into my ear

with each splashing footstep i take

farther from you

i hear nothing of your words

but i see the smile you have discovered

from the performed pouting that was there but a

    minute ago

and that is the shift to goddess

that i witnessed in reverse

the face once taught

against the cool of the morning air

now in motion

and in tune with eyes

full of brightness and abandon

it was only a few steps

before it was likely i would trip

among the loose streambed

and that is what comes to pass

as i reach my hands forward to save my face

and risk my fingers

becoming more broken than even my mind

with my falling

i hear the gasp

not from my own lips

but an echo of you

as my eyes have long since moved from yours

to the fast-approaching ground

and impending taste of soil in my once-white teeth

but when you have gathered what was left of your

      composure

barely left for a second

i make out a single word

between the shock

and laughter

timber

when in my newfound moisture

i turn my head to look up at the sky

now filled with surprised jays

and startled wrens

i see another winged creature hovering

not just at the edge

but nearly centered in my vision

missing a halo but certainly an angel

holding your hand to me

you speak your name

between riotous curls

and laughters broken

only by the difficulty of smiles

and laughs

filling the same mouth at once

and i find myself lifted clear of the water

with a strength i have never possessed within

     myself

i follow

as you leave wet footprints

and cover them with my own bodily drips

to a room not far from that sacred stream

of memories

once wherein i was lost

but now new ones created

of beginnings

and laughters

and smiles

and angelic deliverance

is this what they mean by praying to those winged

     ones above

as if it is

i've been doing it all wrong

till now

wrapped and dry

in a robe only hours taken from your newly-bathed

     self

i sip minty steam

from a camel-decorated mug

and speak soft questions

while you surprise me with speech that feels

     prepared

but can only be spontaneous

thank you

i had forgotten how to laugh

until you came along

and acted the clown

when you didn't even know me

but

from one look

you saw the sadness in my eyes

and took it away

as your lips brush my just-washed cheek

in careful gratitude

i once again learn to smile

and laugh myself

and know in this instant

i have discovered friendship

earth

truth lies cold

at the bottom of the icy stream

leading from a once-solid north but now a

      bahamian wannabe

of liquid separation fences

and passages

where lust

and treasure meet

and greet each other

with a florid wave of their forked tails

doubt

is the beginning of new religions

and the death of old hopes

but in creating new fictions

and telling their stories

as an alternate reality that tastes of gumdrops

and vodka

they have transformed passionate outrage

into bedroom voices

of humanity's own self-deluded mutual fucking

a climate of intensity heats up around us

as we hear raised voices

in time with thermometers

and no longer trees fall in forests

unseen

unheard

unexisting as none still stand

in the face of the flames

we once thought our most important invention

now become our end

as the fires of greed and empire

have mingled with the spinning of centrifuges

to turn us away from the axis of understanding

to one of derision and delusion

where we drink our fill of government koolaid

and swallow once-bitter pills

with sugar-coatings

so think they have become concrete in our mouths

so our tongues no longer scream in fear

we are told to walk

away

from the future

and create a new past we can be proud

of in the image of a well-fired flag

whose stars shimmer with napalm

and zebra lookalikes have rolled in their own

      extinct blood on its torn fabric

to give us the rugs

we once thought were symbols of purity

and native connections

with the world

and now know

simply cover the barren holes in our wild human

      distinctiveness

we have turned

away from our animal need for the world

and pretend it is gone

as we stick our heads in the only sand that is still

  left unformed into bricks

to keep the immigrants out of our flooding cities

and off our unpopulated plantations

and breathe through masks

a haze of hallucinogens

to keep us docile

like the sheep we once thought guided us to a child

  savior

but now lead only to altars of our own

  dinnertimes

we are no longer

one world

one people

one humanity

one existence

one creation even

but we have become one self

one nation under them

not any god of books

or scrolls

or hopes

or fears

or dreams

we worship

ever-changing media images of distinctive sexual

        norms

and think we are liberal

in accepting more than one point of view

so similar in their penetrative provocativeness

and unclothed forms

and naked hatreds

they lead not to the same north

but down toward a hell i once thought fiction

but now created in our image here on earth

as our hard-fired rock of baked clay and molten

        gold

floats through a universe

we only recently began to understand

we forget we can be saved by thoughts

and cling lifelessly to possessions too numerous to
     count
but never sufficient for our own desires

we sacrifice ourselves
and our neighbors
and our children
and our futures
for the grasping fingers of our mind's desires in
     this moment

we torture our fellow lives
and claim to love our animals
because we have caged the bunnies in our
     bedrooms
except for special floppy-eared events
and tie our cutest puppies on the ends of ropes
to keep them from even the appearance of freedom
     they once had
as they roamed the countryside with our death-
     soaked ancestors

who slaughtered each life they happened to
      discover

yet even in their bloodthirsty sport
and self-deluded consumption
of flesh barely stripped from bones before it was
      held to the charcoal of campfires
they took those lives only one at a time
and left the others to learn to fear the human in
      their lands
who had become the predator of predators
and species of unimpassioned cold-bloodedness

and now we kill
not just to satisfy our base desires for taste
but for nothing more than living a life beyond
      comfort
and into a greed
once thought for all but kings
and queens
and emperors

so far beyond the pale it could only be described as

    white

yet we pretend we own this earth

and may control its destiny

by changing our minds

and changing our channels

and changing ourselves to fit with only this

    moment's consumptive obsessions

and that by caring for those no more different

    than our mirrors' faces

we create a better world

and still it burns

as those eyes we turn to only humans within our

    reach

are tightly shut

against the noise that comes to haunt us

in our apocalyptic dreams

and says in the whisper

that is all it has left to give us

stop

silence

twilight calls to me
but i forget how to answer

my tongue remembers
none of the words i was breathing
a second ago
in my own defense
yet the silence and birdsong intermingle
as an ode to a mind
now lost forever

this moment's blackness overwhelms me
but the specks of light
just over the horizon
scream unspoken lyrics
from the stage i've just fallen from

distant stars remind me
of the language of my infancy
when cries turned to awkward questions

then to declarations

of unintended consequences

and faces touched floors one to many times

before i stood

against the garden's young trees

i reached up

to touch leaves newly escaped from their branches

just above my head

and in that instant

i felt

i was no longer a child

and spoke with words

still pitched higher than the clouds

but full of meaning

birds played at my feet

and misunderstood my stares

as interest

when all i searched for

was a way to make my thoughts

take their wings

and learn to be everywhere at once

but i have lost myself
into the quietness of night's echoing shivers
and play guessing games
with my own subconscious

rather than speaking solid truths
i pass on parties
where i am the guest of honor
and dream of invisibility
in the face of panic

no tomorrow
wakes me from the sleep of my unjust nature
but no moon smiles on my rest
so i drink the words on the page
before my eyes
and await the sunrise
to call me from my waking
into quiet time
with pillows

sooner ended than it would have begun

i learned to fly
without the wings of birds or angels
and in the touch of fingers to words
i find myself soaring
through clouds of image
and raindrops of intent

i taste the dreams of water
and swallow the sunshine
from the tops of the haze
as i plunge into the ocean of lost horizons
whose waves i no longer walk on
but hover just beyond

not a second is lost
between the starlight
and its lunar companion
whose lyric lines contain not more than the
        distance
no matter how far it feels

for the weakened light to travel

take this page
and in the light of your face
eat from its depths a banquet of sound
from my lips to yours

breathe deeply
and know within you
not a single letter is missing
from your mirror
held against the life
that dances around you in your waking dreams

take one more step
and close your eyes
to hear your own voice
smile the beauty back into your star-embodied
        eyes

sky

calm is a moment of time

where i free myself

taste myself

breathe myself

in all my beauty

and hate

and thought

and losing what little i dreamed was me

in a new discovery that i make

each time i open not my mouth

but my eyes

as i wonder at the stars floating quickly over my
      head

i take a single heartbeat

to drink in the view

and in this moment

i am truly myself

and nothing outside is pressing itself on me

forcing me to believe

and act

and talk

and accept more than there is within

and in that acceptance i am

and are

and was

and will be the simplest me

and where i am

i cannot help but smile from within the rainbow

that i have drawn on reality

with nothing more than this brush i hold in my

      mind

the sky is falling

yet i manage in a second to catch it

and hold it up

and put the moon and sun back in their place

and nobody else has noticed

that any change has happened

but the bloodless revolution that has taken place

      within me

has shaken me

to the depths of my soul

and broadcast a new me

into the world

where i have no choice but to breathe

and taste

and live myself

through the memories of each spirit i touch

as with a word i walk by

and they smile

and now i look at the mirror i have inside

and know that nothing that has happened in all

      my life

is truly real

beyond that simple smile

field of vision

i am simply amazed

as i sit

a premuddied lotus

to watch the river's embodied life

wander beneath my eyes' hopeful glances

the open sense

as shivering circles dissipate

while raindrops gradually cease their rhythm

and each echo reverberates

undaunted

for endless seconds on the surface

carried downstream

as a transparent leaf on the pull of the moonlight

i sit in the moment

stuck

between sun's softly spoken retreat

in the face of lunar conquest

and the touch of wind blows silent trumpets

whose echoes tear blossoms from the tree above

      my head

only to plunge them onto the liquid empathy

of the surface

kissing them from below

nothing distracts my gaze from the flying dragon

whose twilight search hovers

just above

the reflection

and she searches for her own narcissus

in the beauty of rippled droplets

whose time has only come this instant

her wings craft tiny rainbows with each beat

and invisible fish splash

in the fast-approaching night's quivering

      prediction

yet i feel no queer impressions

from the meters' depth

no marriage

between the states of matter from below

to above

from liquid to breathing

and peace

is kept only by the boundary fence

where dragons penetrate

at their peril and flying fish

dare to flaunt

but only just

and are snatched before my fleeting wink

by hawks

whose presence i could only have a second before

hallucinated into being

the splash of ancient frogs

presages the love of my eyes

plainly redrawn

in words whose meanings are lost to all but the

    poets

as optic ponds are overrun

by flashing floods

and glaciers

overtake the speeding turtles

standing on each other

to reach toward andromeda's distant haze

no twitching brush

captures the moment before me

but i record it

on memory untroubled by chips and logic

as i catch my breath and gasp

as the salts from below

are captured by a nose

unprepared for their presence

no seashore greets me

but the sharpness of my startled realization

captures far too plainly the loss i had been

      wallowing in

as an imaginary body

rotated

reflected in the drops of rain

still hanging in the air

as the gentle wind shakes them

from branches that once kept me dry

but predict my evening shower

with clumsy

abandon

artistic only in its imperfect timing

i see spheres' shadows on once-penetrated surfaces

now calm

in their pacifism

and search there for the story

i may one day be called on to tell

to save this river of delusion from its unowned

    destruction

yet i know it is too late

either for me

or the river

and i realize i know not which of the two will

    disappear

in the morning's overheated glow

while into clouds the water may someday hope

      again to be

in defiance

of its fallen dreams

and prismed existence

yet into ashes

and dust i will be baked

in the glow of fungi

turned to clouds themselves

by the hatred of safety that awaits me

with the sound of the call to prayer

tomorrow's divisions

mark the banks of the river

as it rises beyond sediment

and consumes the tents pitched on its shores

and what once was jumped over in fun

is no longer consumed by sun

but swallows the village it once nourished

as the conqueror biting its feeding hand

with lupine fangs

we trained ourselves to fear

yet in my naive visual meanderings
i cannot give up
hope
in the face of expectations of morning's apocalypse
as the grasshopper at my feet sings for me
as i would never have the talent
to mimic in return

an endless stream of rhythms
perfect without numeric rites
preach stories of lost days
far before we arrived at the bank of any river
to make civilization our withdrawal
or fingers our weapon
to subjugate the trees to our flames
and gills taken from their element to ours
for our all too frigid enjoyment

if in tomorrow's changed climate of lazy
        acceptance

i watch this river swell its empathic hopes for us
to race for conquest
it will only have done it as a mirror
of our own best lessons
on the battlefield
where we sacrifice ourselves
at the altar of discontent
and in the chalice of our own donated blood

in that day
i cannot help but rejoice
as nature returns to herself
and in my burned self-offering
i find the value of return to the beginning
and give thanks for an ending
as poetic as a line wherein i leave the stage

predicted
but still impassioned in my exit line
and in this moment
i look into the river before my eyes
and drink its movement

as no longer can i step not into the same river once

but always be within its waters

not for a second to surface from the sleep i

    searched for

with each beat of the dragon's wings

prayer

collapse into me you young gods

and write through my fingers

the tale of my creation

so i may taste the beginning i once breathed

and remember the time

before i first saw the sun

i write a song of prayer

and sing my shame into the distant planets' paths

where i have no hope

of forgiveness

yet weigh the sins i carry behind my eyes

and find them only feathers

by your hands i feel my life renewed

and as you speak

from your silent lips into my mouth

from distance absent

and passion uncooled

you shiver through me

sensations i had no frame of imagination to
describe
until this moment

the ice of river where once i tripped
and fell
to stand
and fall again
woke me from the sleep of hours of wandering in
sadness
yet no warmth came from the sun that morning
to shield me from the depths of evil i had made
deals with in my soul

but your awakening ice
woke dreams to the surface of my consciousness
and taught me words
in languages i thought
were the preserve of alien tongues
and more distant galaxies' undiscovered bodies
who spoke movement
and talked through minds intertwined

not with sound but sensation

as you have become in me

i come

to be myself in you

as eyes trace the curves

once hidden by white sheets

and fingers

better suited to type voices' memories

follow lines

whose shapes belie the inadequacies of paint

and brush

and canvas

as mere imitations

and not the ephemeral perfection i once believed

    with all my heart they were

yet it was simply my absent discovery

a planting of no flags

in lands that taught me to think of conquests

    undesired

and desires unacknowledged

but with your smile

you called me

past the newly flowing river of contempt

into a garden whose fruits were long since ripened

and lost to the snakes of sunset

entwined within your gaze

i feel warm grass

against my feet

and face

and fingertips

not only mine

and yours

but winds' who carry our laughter out toward the

      trees

onlookers

in a space not truly theirs

yet loaned to us only in this instant

to discover no past

or future

but only us

i sing that song i once had written for the gods
into your lips
as you have taught me they never had the power of
    creation

i found those words that spoke in the beginning in
    your eyes
and found those gods
in the taste of your smile against mine

sanctuary

candles flicker in the half darkness and surround
me with shadows yet i am consumed by
their brightness

they speak words to me that my head hears only as
silence yet they resonate with the truth of
revelation as books have never been able to
do

wooden benches call to me to bow to prostrate
myself between their stone feet and speak
prayers that will never be heard except in
my imagination

whispers of smoke trail toward high ceilings and
distort the colored glass morphing it from
children and lambs and crosses to mirrors
within my heart of who i once was

did i live here at least in spirit once or was it only a

      dream

was my heart a resident of a glass house where no

      stones would be thrown at me or laid over

      my broken face

the lies of my past sleep deep inside a frozen

      ground where snow brings the only trace of

      warmth

yet who am i awake wandering between stone and

      glass if not the hope that once i recognized

      in the morning mirrors as my breath frosted

      their gentle gaze

standing from the stone i make no promises to

      myself yet i dream of tomorrow when i will

      taste the dreams of candles and know they

      will come true

dam

i am crying
i reach out to you and beg your help
pouring my tears into your eyes
as you stare back at me uncomprehending
lost in your own dreams
tasting nothing but the aftertaste of yesterday

you sit by the window staring into the sky
and see the clouds' white faces darken
rain begins gently and reaches into your heart
but runs quickly away and evaporates in the
    daylight

the storm grows with each passing moment
shaking the ground as you watch impassively
safe behind the glass
treating wet rage as calm
breathing in time with the beating of my clouded
    heart

you live in streams of thought while mine seek new

      paths

swelling into rivers

coursing with the blood of new life

brown and green mingling far from where once

      they trickled

but your eyes see nothing as your feet remain dry

natural dams break in the distance

sounds you barely register

that shake you from daytime sleep

not a single moment

and with each passionate downpour

you become more deeply entranced

the water

i send for you

gone viral

brutality attacks me
a dragon in the brightness of solid daylight
as if at night
but it has a face a name a touch i cannot forget
not yours but almost
a shadow of one i remember in my arms
shifted slightly toward the red of anger
walking away without moving your legs
swimming in my drug-soaked veins
as i fight the terror with each swallowed pill
overwhelmed by uncountable terrors
rings around the sun now immigrants within my
    fictitious skin

you are one whose hands once held mine in
    tenderness
body whose touch turned me from connoisseur to
    addict
to junkie wandering in search of corners to find
    the fix

after your bruises drove me into the night

lost to you

while you seek virgin flesh to penetrate with fists

whose fury seethes deep within a shell of sainthood

yet lost causes never truly vanish

and my lips lie awake longing for their missing

      partners

knowing dawn confirms good decisions

while nightingales serenade intentional missteps

and make unrepentant victims of us all

the assault of birdsong from outside my sleep-

      locked eyes

terrorizes me as once your moods scared me into

      pretended morning naps

to face another day without your body your words

      your excuses your touch

i am lost to longing

while i know i would be weak and beg

even in the light of wisdom and daylight

asking for another round whose knockout is

      inevitable

yet i would give in to the flesh that never makes
        the right choice
as no human's ever could
my misery was your design coupled with my
        pleasure
but shattered bones mesh together and blackened
        blues become concealer's cream
as my mind cannot forget but while mind may
        overcome matter
fleshy longings smother it with chemical messages
and make booty-calls whose fingers bear the scars
        of your last show of force

whose eyes are these pressed shut against the dawn
to hold back the longing or the day i have no idea
the impulse to reach out fills the moment
so instead of you i feel inside the nightstand for
        encapsulated warmth
swallowing it rather than your kisses
wrapped in the robe of its aura swimming into me
only to spread out and dull what little feeling i had
        left of life

softening me

another morning passes me by and i am learning

    loneliness by heart

as a new addiction whose drug is safety

they told me once a virus could cure as well as hurt

and i was an unbeliever

hell is the absence of other people

a small price to pay to learn you away

fall

five pointed star

collapse into yourself and depart

leave your gentle perch and leap into the darkness
below

descending to afterlives without a sailor's compass
to guide

yet enfold your arms and clutch your fluid
thoughts

as wind touches your form and blesses you with
tomorrow as a tree

reborn from the ashes of your life's pursuit

the fall that once terrified you

shivering as sunlight's departures stripped
themselves

across an unmistakable gradient of altered time

prismed against a grassy horizon in their left-
behindedness

what feel you

hovering static between this life and unknown

       tomorrows

do you taste the ocean or is it rainbow-frothed salt

to light on

rest against

catching your panicked breath

as ends rush up to meet you

in their stationary hustle

against a backdrop whose name you treat as mud

in humor you only wish was dry

yet in this moment you embody my desire

to step into the river only once and never again

to lift my head and seek a future created by my

       feet against the moisture streaming by

one change is more than plenty to feel alive

before the final shore departs against my eyes

who holds the truth but those whose noises quiver

       with the scent of surrender sharp against

       the terror they once caused themselves

but you let go

beyond yourself and trusted children to the wind

too numerous to count yet absent in the moment

    not yet come

and hope springs not eternal but pouring from the

    river's mouth

as offspring scream their lyrics

against the rushing of the waves

to quench the thirst of dawns you only dream

and in your waking disappear

as do you

yet fall you must

and in that name become my model

standing at the shore become my prison

staring at myself in blackness

reflecting nothing but your voice

calling me to take a single step

along your path

staring

look beyond horizon's dampened relics of the day
as flowers' follies stripped of summer brilliance
rest their feet against your tongue
consumed yet in a moment breathed again
into a night descended early to your eyes
as if their teary hemispheres could even tell

in simulated blackness' filmy shadows rests the
     scent
forgotten by a mind laid bare by trauma's
     sharpened blade
awakened from beneath the surface of
     imagination's lake
to stir to life again the shivering of breathless
     expectation
screaming silently behind clenched lips afraid to
     twitch
yet only still as branches of a distant river
shifting in plain sight with timid reflections to tell
     the tale

awake and breathe and lick the lips of nightmares
		complete another day
swallow their shadows gently as the tar of their
		sinews triggers
desperation you once thought buried resurrected
		in your veins
but momentary drops of past add only flavor to
		the cup of tears
and hold no reins to pull you back to magma from
		within
as overflow avoided calmness falls with the clouds

ice reflects last startling rays as moistened lashes
		brush hands dry with rage
pulse stiller with each beat's near-silent rhythm
as breath returns from gasp to noiseless
		unexcitement
forgetting the chemicals of lost seconds' recent trip
		across the styx and back

horizon calls against the foreground disgusting in
        its humanity
bright with glows of cities inept in their ubiquity
lost to a future once brighter than the lights they
        hold
as if they wandered through unending days
fearful of the night they brought against
        themselves
in lustfilled plays acted on flat-packed stages
built to house the liquid within the newly
        uncovered soul

but darkness saves from sights of others
forgetting their language in ways all too human to
        be animal
yet reveling in excuses of tails once lost and forms
        now become desire
and black against eyes alert to flashes past
        uncivilized ruins not yet destroyed
flickering their call to distant lands where life's
        existence
certain in its presence holds no possibility

of ethics failed so thoroughly as this

below rain-spattered surfaces lie layers untouched
      by adrenaline's rush
silent too in their spoken prayers to gods of steel
      and glass and plastic
yet never still they rise as bubbles from the vents
      beneath a ridge
erupting their ash into the air you once would
      choke on
but sweet enough to tempt a new addiction
and torch the stars to new heights as acid never
      could achieve

childish pleasures appear and fade as seconds tick
      to minutes
yet dolls and simulated treasure hunts hold
      nothing
as sensations of a home now all too far and lost
crash through the glassy look protecting nothing
      but itself

if none but you have skin whose flames dance
        patterns of lost comforts
tomorrow's footsteps still find the path
        illuminated by their shadows' edges

sleep now to wake another day lost to the past
and closer still to living it again
as dreams can be no longer destinations you seek
but flavors of the hope you all but lost until
        horizons called you
with their voices' starshaped whispers in languages
        you forgot you once had known
yet drink as certain smiles with cracks begun but
        showing nothing of themselves
lost for the moments you blindly chose to take
        paths others paved for you
newly sprinkled as with nighttime's absent dew
painted home against the screen behind your soul
awaiting nothing but the sunrise

morning

wake and feel while trying to ignore

the taste of those things better imagined

> disappeared

into the murky realms of sleep behind the mask

you wore through fighting hours against the

> thinly-curtained dark

before it shone a dim reflected light against your

> eyes

not yet detached from tear-drenched blurriness

echoes of images dance just out of reach

but sensations tickle skin and feel as flame on dry

> wood

preparing to consume yet with a touch

strengthening resolve and turning innocence to

> experience

yet in a moment from teacher to killer

what doesn't break may make you stronger

until you have lost your inner self to shivering

> pools of moisture

dripping from the leaking roof of your

    consciousness

into a world whose vicious confrontations

shake the very foundations of your soul

but trouble others only as far as they can drink

    new flavors of the month

trapped within a box not of my own making

but preserved by careful patches grafted from

    within

now unrecognizable as similar to its once-distinct

    form

where doors and windows lived a vibrant life

open for sounds and selves to pass through day by

    day

returning in their pleasured growth

to echo outside voices in head-bound music of the

    night

now live nothing but walls

plastered by fears so logical they feel no assault

    from inside

or out

and screams from a world fall on deaf ears

that shake in terror at the sound

but understand not once a single syllable of their
  argument

as fighting is not for humans

only animals engage

and real humans don't turn the other cheek

standing there to be plowed down by aggressors

too numerous to count

but accepted by their world as justified and
  merited

as strength makes right and the loud survive

the nail that sticks up may be the first to meet the
  hammer

but today the hammer joins forces with the nail

to beat those quiet tacks who in another life

once reveled in their gentle ubiquity

while television screens and tablet videos engage a
  secret hate

felt through the ages but unacknowledged and
  kept beneath the surface

breathes now awake as fires of battle rage

where war was once the answer to all thought

now individuals plot war against the world

one comment at a time

to face the day clothes must depart

only to be replaced by similar straightjackets

accepted not for their specific prescription

but their understanding that speaks a language of

    gender

whose senses stimulate the others in their

    twitching lust

how much to show without appearing to show

    anything at all

a question once answered by convention now

    becomes one of rules to break

as following a trend is now the highest good but

    challenging the boundaries and firmly

    jumping over

is nothing short of praised so where to live

becomes confused

lost in a cloud of wishes for yesterday's twin to

    return

killed before it was born

suffocated by a new rule to be broken

who writes the laws of human behavior

is unknown

as no such sentences exist on paper

yet in the mind to be labelled abnormal is a

      sentence worse than death

for those who live within the confines of a self

      constructed in the image of the land of

      setting suns

to go to battle over mere thoughts is justified in

      their eyes

to hurt and feel no shame

and give in to anger

consumed by hate and passion and most dangerous

      of all pride

in works of others

and a land whose name is nothing more than

      imagined

drawn on paper and screens in languages far

      younger than the species

yet from the bed the time must come

and heads through windows if not doors

when safety screams to stay within the confines of

    the soft

yet others' voices more loudly compel movement

as if compulsive action was their domain alone

and not the result of mouths crammed full and

    swallowed endlessly

if their voices would only stop a moment

their movement turn to stillness

no fears or threats would trap within the bed

or in the house behind the walls built from dreams

    of stone

yet they are unrelenting

continuing their daily circles within spheres of

    brutal influence

whose nightmares simply focus on unintended

    consequences

where once they lost their partners' lust

or failed in their attempts to control the objects of
        another
or others' objectified selves
passionate hatred
of a day without partners and profits
or losing power's stranglehold on the outcomes of
        daily wars

to be an equal in a land of same and silent
is no more than the dream consumed by the
        darkness of the night so recently departed
        into morning screams
as culture rapes itself unwilling to go a day without
        consummation's release
yet stillness is overcome by anxieties too numerous
        to count
with each passing tick toward the necessity to
        engage
one keypress at a time within a land of payback
        and revenge
for thoughts they couldn't possibly understand
as harmony and peace are words they only taste

as music plays and wars are temporarily suspended

and sitting between the trees' stillness drinking

      quiet human absence

frightens them far more than any confrontation

the things they seek

the fights and arguments of their daily lives

provoked intentionally and troubles caused for

      excitement

confused but trained by culture's indoctrination

delivered by schools of mediocrity

and screens of violence

both in their action-packed renditions

but subtly packaged in relationships portrayed as

      normal

with their confrontations and lies and proddings

      and jokes

absorbed as a pattern for an independence more

      prized than acceptance or stillness

while night is darkest and predawn's black calls for

      endless safety between cotton's folds

the day presents itself and is unwilling to wait

regardless of the violence it proposes to unleash

against senses more awake to pain from every noise

    and thought and dream

left latent in its path than any knife could cause

    against its flesh

no sun burns off the heat of morning dread

that lay shaded hours where no nightmare truly

    could inhabit long

the sadness of sleep's failure to refresh is

    incomparable

faced with the certainty of today's world being

    harsher than it once pretended to be

perhaps a moment longer safe within the shell of

    soft

enfolded by armor far more gentle than effective

it may protect from thoughts and fears a little

yet not from the enemy of safety within the self

as digits float unceasingly forward

and awake is now a sentence worse than death

a poison spoken as an arrow

piercing deep inside with each word or movement

they inflict as performance of their daily life

when all desire within is simply stillness

the peace they wish would disappear

quiet of a life they fear

solitude no less complete

than the terror in their darkest nightmare

lost both for lust's unsecret conquest and

      friendship's touch

their half-forgotten torture is my only hope

their dreams ten thousand cuts not merciful

      enough to give me the escape i dream would

      come

damp

peer from beneath your umbrella at eyes clouded

    by rain staring back in the fogged glass and

    smile

day's completion resonates within your heavy head

    with the sound of office ringtones finally

    silenced by absence

candles flicker in the distance calling you forward

    yet you wake to the fact they are nothing

    but moonlight kissing wind-trapped

    raindrops dancing the part of indra's fishing

    gear

pretending to be the planet's yearly cake counters

    in their uncountable team

broken with each twitch of nature's breath yet

    solid as gauze

footsteps sound too high in the near-darkness of

    not-quite-evening but your hat scraping the

    umbrella rim shakes you from passive

    walking

raise your head and unmask yourself to the moist

moment

tongue out stare into the horizon and swallow the

scent of after-the-storm in a mouthful

the park calls you by name drawing you in as no

longer covered you revel joining

unprotected sects of tree worshipers

hugging their deities as liquid streams down

their faces

touch branches and shake their gift of shower

against your fire-kissed hair to bring

refreshment without intoxication back to

your life

sit damp against a ground fit for nothing less

sacred than denim to drink the shapes and

touch pen to page and duplicate now for

tomorrow

no longer disappearing into mists of rain no longer

brushing their leaves but forever etched

a single smile reborn in every breath you take and

gone in a single gasp as wind catches you

unprepared but laugh

cake

footsteps take me to the glade where i feel i could
       have been born
yet unlikely as it sounds
my past was far more traditional and bedded
blood mingling with sheets as cries erupted
and anniversaries started their unceasing count
a morning quick to come yet slow to pass
but in the grass beneath my feet
i stray to imaginings of a life begun here
thoughts dancing with tree offsprings
as they fall to the ground in their windswept
       intercourse
touching each other with less than tender nudges
only to fall to a ground littered with companions
having lost the will to fight or love
whichever they first chose
as if there was a difference

others would contain their desires with cups
yet for me no purse sufficed

and entirety is the better part of valor

as i resolutely take myself to the deep forest

not meaning to consume its honeyed goodness all

      myself

yet in that place to sacrifice it to the deities four-

      footed and nuzzle-prone

if only one would take this sacred day

to baptize me with the waters of the tongue

across my forehead

arrival comes all too soon, the sun not yet setting

      against a backdrop

while the day has burned itself out

against my hopes for its stealthy continuation

yet here i sit

legs crossed between delicate lives

grass tickling parts no other will ever caress

if i get a say in the matter

an issue i all but skirt with its namesake

but lost in reveries is a sudden state

with no border as i sink into its embrace

and an hour loses itself between my eyes

as blue's cousin purple swallows red
and passionately kisses the darkness
as black touches me with its softened antlers

moist softness holds itself just out of reach as i
          contemplate it
but not too long
as temptation tears resistance with its gaze
approaching as i anticipate its sugar
rushing onward to a future of tables underfoot
and notes shaking ears as earthquakes
living in time with bodies bouncing against mine
all in a single breath of sweet abandon
lost to the lust for repetition
while forks dream of my touch
languishing at home as i sit by streaming life

a hand held out attracts rustling
yet i don't expect the pressure suddenly against
          fingertips
instantly there
a family celebrating with me

four hooves good

candles unnecessary yet desirable

as i wish they had made an appearance

yet chocolate quickly disappears and furry

      shadows

descend to the ground and i hear the sounds of

      sleep

shallow at first but trusting the hand that offered

rewards for braveness

my eyes drift closed between new friends

who have always lived just outside my

      consciousness

and i wake to find their footprints in the dawn

as a day no less special in its cakelessness

has begun to cascade through the branches above

      me

and i am free of childish thoughts at last

seen

breathe deeply of galaxies' essence
poured with each passing drop
to satisfy eyes parched of beauty
in a world of grayness and endless streams of
      words

raise fingertips to join midnight arcs
and trace their transformations
across the chalkboard of truncated eternity

drink raindrops from clouds
whose ancestors populated triceratops' horizons
and revel in the delight of tasting a single endless
      loop

pour images of self
against a screen of history
shimmering in a distant field
only to cascade back in myriad echoes
without speaking a single word

walk lanes devoid of memory

and paint stick figures

dancing on the edge of reality

to populate their barren landscapes

of concrete and forgetfulness

listen to the pattern of footfalls

as pavement gives way to grass

descending to pebbles

as toes delight in the lapping tongue

of atlantic abyssals' long-shed tears

hear heaven crack itself

and mold itself anew

in the darkness suddenly shattered

by power no drop of oil could dream of

in a moment of clarity in the silence

broken as bread for your consciousness

to suddenly happen on itself

in reflections of a past

suddenly in the spotlight

inhale shallow fields of vision
and focus their gaze
on the white of newly opened eyes
and lashes shivering in anticipation
of a single leaf falling on the breeze

push air from lungs
trapped decades by societies' imperfect storms
and hear distant harmonies bouncing
in the spinning wind
to find ears finally open to their wisdom

breathe deeply
as galaxies disappear in the brightness of dawn
while eyes finally close
before the credits of beauty
resurrect another moment of dawn

wink

fiction surrounds me as i melt my thoughts to fit
      in the mold i can't stop breathing
todos dance merrily between my ears with
      drunken abandon
yet their footsteps brush against my nose and
      wrinkle it from within
as i place palms together and stretch my soul
      toward the moon's altar
distant music shakes me and i collapse without
      ever leaving my mind

promises lick my lips and move on as once
      unnamed lovers did
leaving nothing for me but lingering strawberries
      and desperate self-abandon
directionless caricatures of myself blending
      without any sense of harmony
lost in myriad holes dispersed throughout the
      chaos of the abyss i call my past

thinly scented with jasmine and crawling with

    regrets' secret venom

my soles walk crosses into a ground fragmented by

    dryness that may or may not be real

yet i imagine it so it can't possibly be otherwise

touch the flood that has risen to my ankles and

    laps against my still-unmoistened sleeves

i command myself to swim yet sink is all i hear in

    the distance

believe i am not stoned and float above the noise

    that tears my ears as gunshots in the mist

fingertips graze the liquid i conjured to protect me

    from my humorless dryness

to laugh with fluent words spoken only in the

    confines of my inner windmills

ceaseless in their turning yet shockingly powerless

    to do more than control my compulsions

dreams will come soon as my face sinks below the

    surface of fictitious waves

and avarice consumes me whole

yet smiles shed their myriad facets on my unveiled
      lips and abandon me to a fate not yet over
i try to breathe the stream but find it suddenly a
      figment of my oasis-deprived state
and pure air pretends to enter my lungs as i taste
      the smoke of humanity torching itself for
      fun
laughter overtakes me and i run without direction
      to jump the gate i only built in my
      daydreams to keep the monsters out

i grab the devil by the shoulders and offer my tears
      to free my soul from these chains
but she turns and i see not horns but my own
      reflection and the links melt in the darkness
as she touches my lips with a finger and points
      inside
i have lost myself but i must be in here somewhere
      sitting on my shoulders pulling strings of
      naughty silk

there was a time i wished i could dive through the
        looking-glass and search
somewhere deep for the self i killed so long ago as
        shame swam through my blood and ate me
        from within
but now i know she was nothing more than
        fragments of my fevered sketches
dancing on overturned tables sheltered from my
        eyes by bloodshot mornings whose
        swallowed memories floated just below the
        surface

now presents give themselves to me as alternate
        pasts to drink with abandon
lies taste of cotton candy and gumdrops while i
        know they are nothing more than populist
        fantasies
elected by children living in a constant state of
        duplicitous bliss and scented smoke rings
awake i scream at myself and the whisper that
        results turns my head toward the sky and i
        open my mouth to speak

yet in this moment a star winks at me and i

    collapse again onto the grass that has been

    holding me up all this time

and run it through my hands as i have never so

    feverishly touched one of flesh

i can't stop staring at the star now fixed in my

    mind as temporary yet my guiding light

hold out my tongue and feel its mint against my

    human raspberry

i close my eyes and know i will awake smelling of

    smiles

about the author

avi has spent their adult life teaching how to write, speak and think in english, turn complex thoughts into beautiful wordplay and communicate with language as the medium. they have worked with native speakers and learners, beginners and professionals. they have hope that someday words will be used to heal the divisions between us rather than hurt and incite to violence and hate. they live beyond the boundaries and divisions of a society trapped in antiquated notions of gender and sexuality but feel compelled to write reflections of that world.

they have lived and studied between canada's east and west coasts, composing poetry on the shores of the atlantic and pacific, holding dear within the heart the solitude that comes from standing at the edge of land with feet no longer willing to turn back toward humanity's lost humanity. they offer this work as a hope that you will take a moment to look at the world around you as perhaps would another, perhaps one without the words to teach you how but the tears to move you to try.

avi invites you to read this work aloud as the mind's voice is never more than a shadow and their joy at spoken words give you the gift of sound only when you breathe it out.

thanks

no writing happens in a vacuum. we often think of our influences. mine have always primarily been classical poets like basho and issa and writers whose work has particularly inspired me to put fingers to keys, tanizaki, dazai, kawabata and gaarder. the language of your medium is far less important than the painting you create with it.

yet it is not all dead writers that make new work possible. as you have gotten this far, i would like to take a moment to thank those who have given me the strength and love to complete this. without the continued encouragement of my parents, i would not have written a single word of this or any other book. bea's insight and aria's questions have kept me on my toes while shoshi's inquisitiveness has stimulated many words to flow. max' and tea's positivity has made sharing a joy and ari, jenn, lucy, waseelah, ashley and ryou have lent me curious eyes when mine were all too tired to see things freshly. finally, shan's, marcela's and sarah's ability to see growth where i often only saw wasted ink has inspired more than they could have imagined at the time.

thank you all.